This is truly the land of the Navajo. Monument Valley was "discovered" by the white man over 55 years ago. Here you will relive the events as our culture found the Navajo's culture. As much as this is a story of the Valley and the Navajo, it is a story of the pioneers: Harry and Mike Goulding, as well as the photographer Josef Muench.

*M*onument Valley is a land of everlasting wealth. The Navajo, the formations, the very color of the earth — all show you a warmth that enriches and excites the emotions.

Monument Valley, *located on the border of northeastern Arizona and southeastern Utah, is a Navajo Tribal Park that preserves scenic values and the Navajo way of life.*

Front cover: Totem Pole and the Yeibichai. This 9 x 12 cm Kodachrome, taken in 1937, is the very first color photograph ever taken by Josef Muench. Inside front cover: John Cly. Page 1: Navajo child with her lamb. Pages 2/3: The Dunes area. Pages 4/5: The Mittens and Merrick Butte; also taken in 1937, this view is the second color photograph ever taken by Josef Muench.

Edited by Maryellen Conner and Cheri Madison.
Book design by K. C. DenDooven.

Ninth Printing, 2004 • Revised Edition

MONUMENT VALLEY: The Story Behind the Scenery.
© 2001 KC PUBLICATIONS, INC.

LC 20-010863. ISBN 0-88714-219-2.

MONUMENT VALLEY
THE STORY BEHIND THE SCENERY®

Photography by Josef Muench.

Josef Muench, who passed away in 1999, came to Monument Valley in 1936, took his first photographs, and returned over 360 times. His sensitivity for the Navajo and love of the land is reflected throughout this book.

Text by K. C. DenDooven.

K. C. DenDooven came to the Valley in 1962 when he first entered the publishing world. Here he met Harry Goulding, who gave him an insight into the magnificence and grandeur of the great Southwest.

Monument Valley Today (pages 44-59) – ***Photography and Text by Bruce Hucko.***
Bruce Hucko — photographer, writer, educator, and children's art coach — focuses on themes of community, art, landscape, and people, and their interrelationships.

This is Monument Valley, a land of profound beauty. Much of the Southwest occupied today by Indian tribes are places the white man didn't want, land he felt to be worthless. Today we all take pleasure in visiting this same land, photographing its rich colors, marveling at its unspoiled beauty. The Navajo and unknown tribes before live with the land. They use it as a source of life.

The Valley has monuments, lots of them. Dramatic sandstone spires, arches, shapes and forms. One could say these magnificent formations have arisen from a sea of sand. Others, more geologically correct, can see the vertical edifices as leftovers after the forces of erosion descended on a sandstone plateau.

This is a land to behold. A land to use with our eyes. It will instill great emotional values. It is a gift from the Creator.

The shape and shadows of Moccasin Arch fulfill its name to all who visit it. Navajos love to be the colorful accents to their proud land.

View from Hunt's Mesa.

The Valley

Everything in life is a matter of perspective. Here we see dramatic sandstone monuments. To the Navajo the Valley is home. To the first-time visitor it is one of the most awesome spectacles of nature he has ever seen. To those of us who have been here many times it is a great place to revisit again and again, a place of beauty and memories — yet a place where we know there is always something more to see and enjoy.

Monument Valley is a land of people, of formations, of mystery and mood. In the winter it can snow enough to literally stop you in your tracks. In the summer it can be very unforgiving to those who don't bring enough water.

The arches and bridges (Harry called them "holes") are just present-day stages in a geologic evolution that started millions of years ago and will continue on forever.

THE DESERT

At a quick glance this land looks like a dry, dusty, barren desert. Desert it is — but with life all around you. The Navajo live here in a world that is theirs. They raise families and tend sheep. There is water; trees and flowers do grow; children have fun, go to school, work, play. The desert floor teems with life — you just have to look for it.

Back in 1938, Hollywood was astounded to find out that there *was* a real West, complete with real, live Indians. They could leave their make-believe back lots and produce movies in the *real* West. "Stagecoach" was shot here. A young actor by the name of John

"Nowhere in the world can one find a similar effect of nature's work. Words alone, the thousand-foot pyramid and castles, the slender tower, bridges and arches — cannot begin to describe the sandstone formations that dominate Monument Valley."

Josef Muench.

Wayne would be discovered. Director John Ford would find his "point." Western towns would appear (and disappear) — but more of that later.

Visiting Monument Valley is a great experience for there is much to be seen. As you go over the next hill or around the next bend a unique world unfolds in front of you. Besides an extraordinary geologic history there is a great human history that goes well back in time, even before the Navajo. We will not understand everything we see here in just one tour or one experience. Those who can return again and again do so because it is a land of intrigue.

The present-day scene is a little different than it was in the late '30s. The Navajo have traded in their wood-spoked wagons for pickup trucks. The road to Monument Valley is now paved. Now there are air-conditioned motels with all the modern trappings.

NAVAJO TRIBAL PARK

This is a Navajo Tribal Park. The tribe maintains a visitor center, monitors tours into the Valley, and patrols the area so it will be enjoyable for those here today and preserved for those who will come next year and in future decades.

But the mood of the people and the look of the proud rugged land is always here. You get a sense of adventure even as you drive down the highway adjacent to Monument Valley. Actually, the Arizona-Utah state line runs just about through the middle. Who cares? Nature didn't. The Navajo doesn't. Monument Valley is here, to be shared and viewed by all.

Navajo horsemen add the feeling of presence to the dramatic North Window.

A Valley Full of Arches

▲ *Full Moon Arch is typical of the open formations in Monument Valley. It is a present-day statement in an involved geologic process. Nature finds a weak spot in the thin sandstone cliff. Be it a crack or a small hole in the vertical face, the elements drive against the rock to open the sandstone to daylight and sky. Winter rain and snow followed by freezing and thawing work the cracks till larger chunks fall out. But always it's the wind and blowing sand that rounds off the edges. Will it last? No, it's just a phase. When the top collapses we'll see a U-shaped opening. In time the entire wall will come down as the geologic process happens and moves on.*

Called Swinnerton ▶ *Bridge, this high-up formation was named after the artist/ cartoonist Jimmy Swinnerton. Names applied to virtually all the formations in Monument Valley are the white man's view of things. Sure the Navajo have names for these places, but — in Navajo!*

◀ *Hidden Bridge shows evidence of the water flowing over and through the opening. To those who wonder, a bridge is a rock span that was undercut by a flow of water. An arch is a span created by weathering, like Full Moon Arch on the opposite page.*

Sheep - Wool - The Way of Life

The Navajo's life in Monument Valley revolves around sheep more than any other single entity. The two main trading commodities of the Navajo are wool and woven rugs. Both are products regenerated annually from their flocks of sheep. The land simply will not support enough grass for great numbers of sheep to be raised and sold like cattle.

In years past people brought wool to Goulding's Trading Post to buy commodities. Today they are more apt to take the wool to a larger city in pickups. While it is a time-consuming process, some of the wool is woven into beautiful Navajo rugs, especially during the long winter months. Just the presence of the sheep themselves is of economic value. They are photographed daily being driven down sand dunes in areas seen by visitors (pages 2/3). Sheep and goats are also a source of food.

▲ **Springtime means shearing time. It's always a family** affair and the sheep are treated carefully, almost like pets, for their wool will be needed again and again. It may seem hard for a first-time visitor to believe, but this is the very beginning of a beautiful and valuable Navajo rug.

...and Flowers Too

◀ **If you ever wondered** about the "purple sage" in western tales, well, this is it. The red sands provide an even more dramatic background. Like all the plants, flowers, and trees in the Valley they grow when and where there is adequate moisture. The root system draws up what it needs. If there's not enough rainfall this year the plant goes dormant. It doesn't die. Sudden rain will make the desert bloom again in a myriad of shapes and colors.

*◀ **F**ew large trees grow in Monument Valley. There just isn't enough water to support many. This silhouetted cottonwood is an exception. Navajos prefer not to camp or stay close to a tree. They feel their presence disrupts the root system. Also, maybe they know more about lightning strikes than we do!*

***S**nakewood ▶*
gets its name for good reason. The Navajo know to give it proper respect since the dense bush makes an ideal spot for a rattlesnake to get away from the intense sun.

*◀ **C**liffrose*
supplies more than just a pretty subject to photograph. The shrub beneath the blossoms is called babybrush by the Navajo since they use its shredded bark as a soft mattress in their babies' cradleboards. In back, one of the Mittens dominates the skyline with its bold presence.

*◀ **C**ontrast.*
The brilliant red signifies this as a low spot where moisture and fine silt collect. The rocks in the Valley really are this red. A small rabbitbrush accents the background.

Mystery Valley — Land of Intrigue

▲ **W**hat dramatic views you can get in Monument Valley by combining unique formations with the proper camera angle. A double arch can be a sinister face. Who has more fun, nature or the photographer?

◄ **H**alf-moon Arch. Another name created by our imagination. There is a small ruin under the far side of the archway which will accommodate just two people. If the white man had built it, he probably would have put it out in front and in the center. The Anasazi knew better. He located the dwelling off to the side so it wouldn't be seen by an enemy or washed away by the next flash flood.

▲ **Honeymoon Arch,**
in Mystery Valley,
presents a feeling of
balance and symmetry.
Harry, who found this
formation decades ago,
provides human
scale to show off
the size of the arch.

Caves provide not only ▶
shelter from the elements, but
they can be adapted into homes,
granaries, and at times be set up
for religious purposes. Again,
this site is in Mystery Valley.

▲ *Flash flood — an awesome sight in the Southwest. Rain clouds off in the distance can produce a driving river down into an area where the sun still shines brightly.*

The Forces of Nature that Created the Land

The Three ▶
Sisters refer to three nuns, not three siblings. Here it's easy to see the two mature nuns leading the thin young initiate between them. Isn't creative imagination wonderful!

Sometimes called ▶
El Capitan, this 1,400-foot-high volcanic plug is a remnant of the intense volcanic action that took place in the Southwest. What we see here is the hard center core of a volcano after the softer outer rocks have been eroded away. Wind and water are the forces that have carved everything we see in the Valley. The Navajo call this the Agathlan, which means "The place of the scraping of the hides." Here, periodically, the sheep are shorn of their wool, and the people of the Valley enjoy a pow-wow (a social gathering and celebration).

"Happy" Cly grooms the hair of her husband, Willie Cly.

The Navajo is one of the most interesting tribes to observe and learn about. They are by far the largest Indian tribe in North America. More than 180,000 live on their Reservation which is about the size of West Virginia. Window Rock, the capital, is the closest to what you'd call a city. Kayenta, just south of Monument Valley, is more typical of the towns within their land. They call their Reservation The Navajo Nation, and in many ways they do operate like a small independent country surrounded by a very large country.

Navajos are nomads and adapters. They live off the land. They live by their rules and at their own pace — both of which in many ways are distinctly different from the white man's. Sheep and wool are one of the main forms of industry throughout the entire Navajo land. Sheep wander — Navajos wander, and both live where the conditions are workable.

Their entire history shows a life style of adaptation. Their language is derived from the Athabascan-speaking tribes of northwest Canada. Much of their agriculture relates back to the Apache and Pueblo Indians. Yet they

> *"This atmosphere is not a figment of the imagination. Here is a blend of cultures from deep-rooted ways of the ancient ones to pickup trucks and self-winding watches. Colorfully dressed women match the beauty of the red sandstone in which they live. Monument Valley is their home."*
>
> *Josef Muench.*

do not build stone homes. Their hogan (hō-gän) is a well-engineered home for the desert, cool in the summer — warm in the winter.

When the Spaniards arrived with horses, it made sense to the Navajo so they adapted the horse, or more correctly the Navajo pony which is a lighter-weight, somewhat short-legged horse. The wood-spoked wagon was fine until the development of the pickup truck. Today a wagon's only use is for photographers, parades, and to show visitors what life was like in the "old days."

They believe in the Medicine Man. He still performs healing ceremonies, but they will also go to the Monument Valley Hospital. Many Navajos when sick play it safe — go to the hospital *and* see the Medicine Man.

Navajo Rugs

Navajo rugs are prized for their quality and beauty. The money the Indians get for selling a Navajo rug may well be used for buying a Pendleton blanket since it's warmer. Many of their arts and crafts (rugs, silver and turquoise, decorated baskets and pottery) came about because traders such as Harry Goulding pointed out that they could earn money by making quality arts and crafts.

Here in Monument Valley you see the Navajo as he lives today, but with reminders of the way of life as it has evolved over the last 50 years. Roads to get to the Valley are now paved. But roads in the Valley vary from graded gravel to four-wheel-drive (requiring Navajo guides), to just hiking trails.

Perhaps it could be said best that Monument Valley serves as their showplace. The Navajo's window into their unique world. They are proud of their land — and rightly so. It has a beauty and majesty all of its own. Here you are a visitor to the life-style of the Navajo.

A Navajo family ▶
in front of The Three Sisters. Hogans always face the east. This is both tradition and a practical use of the sunrise's warming rays. The sheep are normally out in the Valley. Horses are still very much in use. The photogenic rug loom is generally outside the hogan except in winter or bad weather.

▲ ***R**ug weaving inside the hogan. The raw wool* next to the mother is being cleaned and carded by the daughter. Both will work at dyeing wool and spinning it into usable yarn. The prep work to get wool ready for weaving is often longer than it takes to weave the rug. This pattern is more modern than the one seen on the opposite page or below.

◄ ***T**he Two Gray* Hills rug is typical of those made in the eastern part of the Reservation. Most weavers produce a great variety of patterns depending on their mood or the requests placed by traders.

K.C. DEN DOOVEN

▲ **In summer a family will live and work in a covered shelter, usually close to their** hogan. If the best area for their sheep is a bit too far away, they will establish a "summer home" close to the flocks. Life on the Reservation is very much a family affair with all members working together.

The difficulty the Navajo, in fact all Indian tribes, face is that money and jobs lie outside in the white man's world. But their culture, roots, and families are still back on their own land. So, they tend to go back and forth to try and balance their monetary needs with their spiritual needs. It is a very real and very complex problem.

Overleaf: One of ▶
the many moods of
the Valley, from
Hunt's Mesa
(compare with page 8).

23

Dineh: The People

◀ **A** *Navajo woman, her blouse bedecked with silver and beadwork of the '40s, stands in front of a partially completed storm-pattern rug. The coins are dimes which adapt well as decoration jewelry. Quarters and half-dollars were used, but usually not silver dollars (cost? weight?). The silver and turquoise they wore was their "bank." Where else could they keep their wealth? No banks here, and paper money did not seem real. Consider the "buying power" of a quality turquoise and silver necklace.*

The cradleboard ▶ *was a practical invention of the Indian people. A loop at the top provided a sun shield when the mother carried the child on her back. The board could be set down without disturbing a sleeping baby. Babybrush was used inside for padding — the original biodegradable solution to an age-old situation.*

▲ *The look of age and wisdom. Taken* in the '40s, this photograph by Josef Muench illustrates much of the Navajo's outlook back then.

▲ *The velveteen blouse and satin skirt with silver and* turquoise were proper attire to be worn for photographers.

The lives of a ▶ *young girl and her mother were busy and provided a lot of closeness as they worked and played together. The daughter helped card wool, learned to cook and sew, and watched after the sheep, unless there was an older brother to do this.*

27

Anasazi Petroglyphs &Pictographs

▲ **A**n ancient pot unearthed by the shifting sand and photographed in 1963 exactly where it was found.

◄ **P**etroglyphs — why here? The same reason humans do things in specific places — for a specific reason. This was dry desert country even 10,000 years ago. Eking out a life was difficult — no time for meaningless doodles. This is rock writing. Inscriptions to convey information to be read and understood. We need to preserve this and learn more about its intended message.

Kay-tso, an old ▶ Medicine Man, shows a section of a large panel in the Valley. Rock writing stopped about the time of the coming of the white man. Indians back then were unsure who they could trust (they still are!). Today few of any of the tribes can read petroglyphs. The study of just what information was recorded is a present-day challenge.

Pictographs, that is painted images, come close to being an art form. The hand symbols were used in many areas and could be an ancient way of saying "I was born here." These markings in Mystery Valley have stood centuries of time. Too bad our modern house paint and printing ink can't be as good!

There are not many large ruins in Monument Valley. These are just south of the Valley proper, toward Kayenta. The formations in Monument Valley did not produce too many large natural caves or overhangs. The techniques of construction are fairly common throughout the Southwest. Mesa Verde, Canyon de Chelly, Chaco, and the Navajo National Monument all have larger dwelling sites.

Sand Painting and a Healing Ceremony

Sand paintings were created as part of a healing ceremony performed by the Medicine Man — usually an elder in the village or area. While he uses herbs and natural plants, the sand painting ceremony is more like a form of prayer. In a case like this photo sequence the man is healing the mind, cleansing the soul.

▲ **F**irst the ground must be ▶ *prepared. Special fine sand is brought in to be spread on the smooth ground. The girl up on the hillside with her family watches the Medicine Man making his preparations. This girl was tending a flock of sheep when a rattlesnake crossed her path. It did not bite her, but she needs the ceremony to take away fear, take away any worries that the snake will return.*

◀ **A**fter the various *colored rocks are ground up (above) the design is made. Here we see the Yei figures. A Yei is a masked representative of a supernatural being which possesses great power. Over 600 different designs are used in sand paintings, depending on the need.*

▲ **The girl now sits in the middle of the sand painting. This is her ceremony. The Medicine** *Man will do chants, and communicate to the Yeibichai figures in Navajo mythology. He has a medicine bundle from which he has drawn elements to help the healing process. The girl, and her family, has total faith in this man to remove the mental and emotional cloud so that she can go forward and not worry about any evil happening from the past event. Seldom are outsiders allowed to photograph an actual healing ceremony. Josef Muench's long years of work with the Navajo, especially at Monument Valley, gave him the opportunity to take these pictures in 1960. Once completed the painting will be destroyed, and the sand collected to be taken back to where it was originally obtained.*

Harry and Mike in 1945.

"Let me call you 'Mike'." — Harry Goulding was moving into this Arizona/Utah country to establish a new life with his new bride. Her given name was just too much for him to remember. He had sheep to take care of, household effects to move across the desert. They were moving into a land where nobody spoke English. So, Mike it was — now he could concentrate on his other problems.

Born in Durango, Colorado, in 1897, he moved from a ranch near Aztec, New Mexico, to Monument Valley in 1923. A Model-T made the journey across the sandy desert. Roads then, at best, were little more than trails. A sheepherder by trade, Harry lived off the land, just like the Navajo. He established the trading post and began to set down his roots.

Not only did Harry and Mike understand and befriend the Navajo through a half-century of business, but they really are the people who brought Monument Valley to the world. Perhaps it would be better to say they brought the world to Monument Valley.

Subsequent to their arrival in the Valley, the stock market crash of '29 wiped out nearly any chance for business. The Valley was there, the Navajo lived off the land, but Harry needed to find a monetary source. The solution presented itself in the late '30s when Harry learned that Hollywood was going to make a western movie to be called "Stagecoach." He decided he'd be a one-person ambassador for the Valley.

"Stagecoach" Arrives

And he did it! After "Stagecoach," "My Darling Clementine," "She Wore a Yellow Ribbon," "Fort Apache," "The Searchers," and many more were shot on location in the

> *"Like the fine rugs that the Navajo women weave, so too are the finest of people associated with Monument Valley — Harry and Mike (Leona) Goulding. They settled here as traders in 1923 and put names to many of the monuments in this, the heart of Navajoland."*
>
> *Josef Muench.*

Valley. Movie companies hired Navajos and spent a lot of money. This was only the beginning.

Harry's work directly and indirectly led to many friendships such as with Josef Muench whose photos in "Arizona Highways" magazine publicized the Valley. Lots of magazine articles both in this country and throughout the world started to tell about this extraordinary land.

If you never saw Monument Valley, but only photos of it, you'd wonder if this place was for real. Even after Hollywood made the decision in 1938 based on Josef's photos, they still chartered a plane to see for themselves that this Valley and its monuments really existed.

Those who knew Harry and Mike knew their love and respect for the Navajo was very profound. Not only did they want to bring people to see the Valley and to help the local Indians become employed, they also worried about the Navajo's health.

Harry knew the Medicine Men and respected their value. Harry also knew a modern hospital and doctors were needed. In the '60s he arranged for the Seventh-Day Adventists to build and establish a hospital just around the bend from his trading post. He leased them the land for $1 per year on a 99-year lease, and then gave much personal financial support.

People don't start life with a game plan or purpose — it evolves, it happens. Harry had a calling to live among and help the Navajo people. Mike shared it with him each and every day. Josef Muench had a calling to be a photographer. Although he has taken many dramatic photographs all over the world, perhaps his greatest work was a small, 8x10 black and white album done back in 1938.

Goulding's Trading ▶
Post was designed and built by Harry and Mike in 1928. The Navajos who helped them had never before seen a two-story stone building. Today the post is a recognized national landmark as well as a functioning museum in the same trading-post style that served the Navajo for over 60 years.

▲ **_Two Navajo women and their ponies stand on Ford's Point. This is the spot where_**
director John Ford liked to set his camera to capture a Navajo on horseback or the "hero" out on the point to the right. Visitors often mistake the actor's place for "the" Ford's Point.

_**Tombstone,** ▷
Arizona, as it was rebuilt in Monument Valley, Arizona — for the movie "My Darling Clementine." Just for the record, all the magnificent background is in Utah. Sets like this are completely removed after a movie is shot. The desert lives on._

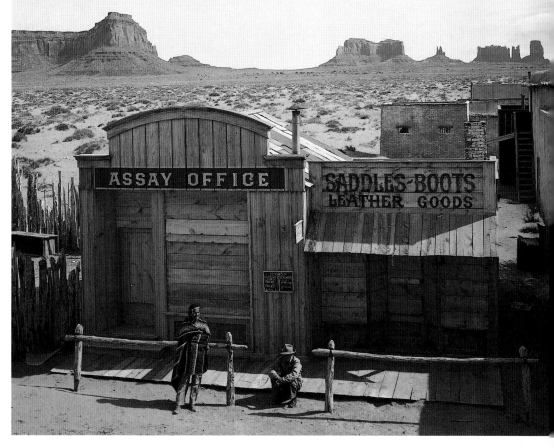

The Movies Come to Monument Valley

"Stagecoach": 1938

Harry knew something had to be done. There was no money, no income, no future. The scenery was fabulous but nobody ever saw it. He told Josef Muench he planned to go to Hollywood to convince them to use the Valley to make movies.

Harry was going to use simple snapshots that people had sent him — box camera stuff. Josef knew Harry would never succeed with those photos. He said he'd make up a special album of black and white pictures (color film was just invented, Hollywood wasn't using it yet). So off Harry and Mike went — with canned goods from the shelves of their trading post for food enroute.

When the receptionist at United Artists gave Harry a brush-off he told her that was OK, he'd brought a bedroll and would just roll it out in the lobby! Harry always was a very patient man. To get rid of him, a location manager came to the lobby. One look at the photos and off he went with the pictures. A bit later the photographs were laid out in front of John Ford and production chief Walter Wanger, with Harry describing the Valley.

Hollywood was in its flamboyant era. Top men made decisions on the spot. Committees hadn't been invented yet! Within a few hours the die was cast. Monument Valley *was* the place.

Parts of Harry's story tell a lot about him and the era. Wanger said that he'd contact Babbitts in Flagstaff to arrange for needed supplies to be shipped to the Valley. (By the way, at that time the paved road stopped at Tuba City.) Ford and Wanger said that Harry would also need money for things to have on hand. So they gave him a check which he just folded and put in his pocket.

On their way back to the Valley, in Williams, Arizona, Harry and Mike ran low on gas — not enough to make it to Flagstaff, 33 miles east. "No problem," said Harry, "they gave me a check." And he pulled into a local gas station. Remember this was in 1938, the depression era. The check made out to Harry was for *Five Thousand Dollars!* The station man said it was the best laugh he had had in ages, gave Harry two gallons, and sent him on his way.

When Harry and Mike did arrive in Flagstaff they saw a long run of stake trucks lined up on both sides of the street in front of Babbitt Brothers General Store. Harry met Ed Babbitt out in front and asked, "What's going on?" "Harry, you tell me what's going on — Hollywood is on the phone every half-hour adding to the list of items to be shipped to the Valley."

And thus the Valley was discovered for all to see, in person or in movie houses worldwide.

▲ *Harry, back in the '40s, dealing with a Navajo woman. Note her Pendleton blanket.*
Sometimes things were bought with actual cash money, but more often barter or credit was the form of transfer. Turquoise and silver jewelry could be pawned, to be paid off when the sheared wool was brought in or Navajo rugs were delivered to the trading post. Harry virtually never sold a pawned item.

Maurice Knee starts ▷
to fill an order at the counter. A trading post was far more than just a country store. It was where people met, exchanged local news, learned what else was happening in the world (if they cared!). Problems were solved, and disagreements settled. A good trader was a respected judge and jury in these remote areas.

Family

In the living room ▶ at the trading post the family gathers. Left to right: Mike; Harry; Maurice (Mike's brother); Mrs. Knee (mother of Maurice and Mike); and Harry's Aunt Molly. It took unique people to live and operate back in the '40s-'50s. Morris Knee's brother Lurt Knee and his wife operated the lodge at the south end of Capitol Reef. Harry was a distant cousin to Art Greene who started the operations at Wahweap, before there was a Lake Powell. (Note: The photo over the fireplace is one of Josef Muench's.)

▼ **Harry and Mike had to be morning people. Their home faced the east, like a hogan. Sunrises** signaled the beginning of a brand new day. Their life had to be a great adventure. They did what they wanted to do, when it needed to be done. They answered only to the supreme being of life and the orderly balance of nature. This is the scene they enjoyed each morning, and ultimately brought the world to Monument Valley so it could be shared.

Josef Muench working with one of his favorite subjects.

Josef Muench

Josef G. Muench — a man who at age 23, in 1927, actually hit Adolph Hitler with a tomato he threw, and lived to tell the story — is not just the photographer of this book; he is almost as much a part of the Monument Valley story as Harry and Mike Goulding.

Each of us is a part of the great scene. Harry and his Navajo friends lived the Valley. But until Josef's photos appeared in "Arizona Highways" and his work was spread out in Walter Wanger's Hollywood office — the Valley was unknown, unseen, and unvisited.

Like most intriguing stories, the beginning is far away. Josef was born February 8, 1904, in Schweinfurt, Germany. When he was 12 his mother gave him his first camera, a simple box style she had received from her employer at Christmas.

Taking photos of friends and selling them the pictures for pennies allowed Josef to buy his next camera for ten marks (about $10.00 then). He was on his way to his destiny.

JOSEF MOVES TO AMERICA

At the Hitler incident there had been S.S. officers sitting on both sides. Hitler was just an emerging radical then, but Josef knew when he and his followers came to power they would remember his defiance. He would be a marked man. So, Josef left his homeland and came to the United States in 1928, and got a job with the Ford Motor Company.

The urge to see the entire United States was great. As soon as he could afford a Model-A roadster ($535, cash) and save up $300 for travelling money, Josef headed west.

Reaching Santa Barbara, California, on

"Having seen that Desertscape now hundreds of times, it is no longer possible to remember what it looked like the first time. I can no longer capture a state of mind in which Monument Valley was not a part of my mental and emotional equipment."

Josef Muench.

November 15, 1930, he decided that this would be his new home. The swaying palms and breaking surf were just too appealing for Josef to look elsewhere.

Taking photographs was his love, his life, his future. But, in 1930, with a 25-percent unemployment figure, his more pragmatic side told Josef to take a job as a gardener at St. Francis Hospital. Today his home, the same one he bought in '34, is a good display of his gardening skills.

His first commercial sale was an 8x10 black and white photo of a bus for a cover on "Trailways Magazine." $5.00 in 1931. He was back on the trail to his destiny.

"ARIZONA HIGHWAYS," THE VALLEY, AND KODACHROME

Josef met Raymond Carlson, the driving force who turned "Arizona Highways" from a state road construction magazine into today's very well known scenic publication. Josef left Raymond fifty 8x10 black and whites to review in '36. Eventually the magazine published every one of those photographs.

After his first trip to Monument Valley in 1935, he returned with his wife, Joyce, in '37. Joyce was a writer, so the two teamed up on a story about the Valley which appeared in "Arizona Highways" in '39.

Eastman Kodak came out with Kodachrome in 1937. In that year Josef shot his first color photograph. Where else?! (It is this book's cover photo.) In working on this Monument Valley book Josef made his 354th trip into the Valley, at age 87. His love and respect for the Navajo, Harry Goulding, and the Valley never diminished. Josef lived to the age of 95, still searching for his best photograph.

▼ **In the '40s the roads into the Valley were a couple of ruts in a sandy trail. The wildflowers** blossomed, the Navajo lived their way of life, and Monument Valley was about to be rediscovered.

The Navajos in Their Valley

◀ **J**osef enjoys his relationship with the Navajo. Who else could get them to bring out their own simple cameras to pose for a photo. Now if only we could see what they were taking a picture of — tourists or scenery?

Lunch time in ▶ the Valley. The Navajo has very strong family ties. The man on the left is not a relative, but since he had no family he's been "adopted" by the others. This is the way of the Indians, they recognize one's need for being part of a family.

▲ **M**onument Valley is a photographer's (or movie maker's) dream come true. The spires, the clouds, the clean air, the open spaces, the colorful Navajos, the ponies, the sheep, the sand dunes — all of these are elements that individually make for good picture material. Here they can be combined into one single photograph!

People who return time after time feel cheated if the sky is cloudless. The patterns created on the Valley floor, the monuments that dance in and out of the shadows are such that from a single spot you can shoot many different pictures in a matter of minutes.

The North Window is a favorite of all photographers, from those with a simple camera to movie directors and ad-agency executives. The Navajo are very used to being photographed. Some are sort of pros who feel they should be paid to have their picture taken. And why not? — They are being used as models. Even their horses know how to pose. Kodak today still uses the Valley as a subject to demonstrate the quality of its film. They know that Monument Valley is one of the most photographed sites anywhere in the world. And rightly so.

Working with Light - Snow - People - A Love of the Land

Harry and ▲ one of his Navajo friends talk about "their" Valley. A natural setting in this dramatic country.

◀ **There are some** unique areas in the Valley that require searching out. Rooster Rock in front of the thousand-foot-high Meridian Butte is just one of these special places.

Yes, it does snow ▲
in the Valley. Occasionally
up to three or four feet.
A light blanket of the
white stuff is great to
accent the form and color
of this red-rock country.

In the '40s this ▶
was the view from the
trading post's front
door. The stone
building was reserved
for John Ford when he
was there either to
shoot a move or just
relax and enjoy
the Valley.

Monument Valley Today

by Bruce Hucko

Monument Valley is an ancient land where children grow in traditional and modern ways. "The valley gives me a spiritual connection to my ancestors. I've never met them, but I can feel them," states Laticia Rodriguez, Homecoming Queen 2000.

The landscape of Monument Valley is one of timeless beauty and mystery. The sandstone spires and buttes that give this land its name have stood seemingly unchanged for eons. The winds blow, sand dunes shift, water freezes, a rock cracks and falls. Though the land is constantly being eroded, the change is so slight as to be unnoticed.

By contrast the human element has changed greatly. Once the sole refuge for Navajo families and their livestock, Monument Valley is now a destination point for domestic and international tourists, Hollywood film crews, magazine writers, and countless photographers. Visitation has increased 1,000 percent from the 1950s to 2000.

Monument Valley Tribal Park occupies 91,696 acres on the Utah-Arizona border. From the visitor center one can see most of the features, take a 17-stop, self-guided driving tour on dirt roads, or contract a Navajo guide service for visits to special, non-public areas.

Monument Valley is no longer remote. Tour busses, airlines, and a paved highway bring more than a half million visitors here annually.

No matter how you arrive, once you enter Monument Valley Tribal Park you are immediately transported into another time and place. Pavement turns to rutted dirt roads, open doors reveal usually hot dry air, and your skin is soon coated with windblown sand. These are not hardships, but part of the beauty of life here.

At Monument Valley you meet nature on her terms, not your own. And the rewards for doing so are great. First there is the beauty of light and rock. Get up for sunrise and don't miss sunsets!

"The love of the Navajo people for their land seems to seep out of every rock and bush. It is in every smile, and despite many daily hardships it still persists. By visiting here you become blessed — with a child's laugh, an elder's greeting, the touch of ephemeral sunlight upon the timeless rock. "

Bruce Hucko.

The pace is slower here. Absorb it. Take time to sit and savor what your senses are experiencing. Many visitors stay but a few hours. Consider a few days with time given to touring, walking, and just sitting on a rock.

The best reward of all, however, is to talk to local Navajos where you may learn to see and feel about Monument Valley as Navajos do — as a land of living rock and spirit, where one's actions and thoughts are guided by a close relationship with the forces of nature. At first reticent, after some time spent together, most valley residents and guides are quite willing to share their love of the land, their culture, and their special brand of humor with you.

In order to continue living in the valley, families have let go of the traditional economy of livestock and trading and have adapted to the pressures and needs of the tourist industry. Several families maintain booths at featured overlooks, displaying a variety of native jewelry and often posing for photographs. A few charge a small fee to visit a traditional hogan or to view a rug weaving demonstration. Sheep no longer run over the dunes by the Totem Pole unless they are getting paid by commercial photographers. The water there has gone salty.

A Sharing of the Land

In addition to sharing the beautiful landscape of Monument Valley with tourists, valley residents compose a small community of Navajo people trying to create and maintain a life in a land they love. Valley residents have chosen to live without electricity, running water, and close shopping. Wood for heat and hogan building comes from mountains 75 miles away. Area residents must drive their children dozens of miles daily on dirt roads to meet the school bus, purchase groceries, go to work, or receive health treatment. The nearest "cities" — Moab, Cortez, Shiprock, Gallup, or Flagstaff — are each over one hundred miles away.

Valley residents are resilient and independent, and take great pride in where they live. Most current residents live on the land their grandparents and elder ancestors settled. When you drive or tour here, you are not just visiting another public park, but a landscape that the Navajo know as home. The Navajo share their "backyard" with you. More than a beautiful place, Monument Valley is sacred to the Navajo people. Valley residents are the true guardians of that trust.

Ted Cly is 75 years ▶ *young. The son of Willie and Wanda "Happy" Cly (page 20), he guided tourists for 38 years and was the primary guide for Josef Muench. "I was raised here so I know where everything is!" he says proudly. "I took him everywhere!"*

◀ **This is a** landscape of mythic proportion and fame. Thanks first to John Ford and John Wayne and later to a growing list of international commercials and Hollywood films such as "Back to the The Future III," Monument Valley has become the symbol of the American West for people worldwide.

Tours Abound

◀ **One of the most rewarding ways of** experiencing Monument Valley is to take a guided horseback or jeep tour. Over one dozen Navajo-owned and operated companies offer tours of the valley and adjacent lands. With them you are able to visit arches, ruins, and rock art that the general public cannot. Each guide provides well-informed, cultural, historical, and geologic information. Individual guides often play traditional Indian flute or drum and sing, or share cultural stories at prime locations. They all tend to be good natured and willing to share their knowledge of Navajo culture.

▲ **Navajo guides take pride in**
◀ educating tourists about their culture. "Navajo religion teaches about nature," states David Lee Clark (above). "The rocks speak to Navajo people. We ask them for rain and other blessings using songs and prayers." "Our elders have a lot of respect for every one of these monuments," says Roy Black at Tear Drop arch (left). "They are all sacred, and that is something we can share."

Navajo Life

◀ **M**onument Valley Tribal Park is one of eight parks operated by the Navajo Tribe. Managing them much like United States national parks or monuments, the Navajo have the unique challenge of managing tourism in a land where people have continued to live for decades.

The tourism business offers local Navajos the ability to live and provide for their family in the land they love. Paying for a guided tour helps feed and employ several families — and may just save you a large mechanic's bill later on! ▼

in the Valley Today

Beauty is an important ▶ concept and practice in the Navajo way of life. Wearing silver and turquoise is a sign to others that you acknowledge beauty in your life. After enjoying the natural beauty, many visitors purchase rings, bracelets, and other objects from vendors with a business location that is hard to beat. Here a Navajo girl meets people from all over the world and helps support her mother and sisters by tending to the family's jewelry stand at John Ford Point.

◀ **L**ifetime valley resident Jerry Cly owns and operates a jewelry outlet at North Window. He recalls the day the valley called him home from California. "One day in really slow traffic, my eyes got real stingy. I had tears. I could smell the smog. Right then I started thinking about coming back," he says. "When I did, it was overwhelming! To see the blue sky and the beauty was just totally awesome. I started taking pictures just like tourists do. Now I know why they come here."

▲ **As children of weaver Susie Yazzie, Lonnie and Effie Yazzie have learned to value their** Navajo upbringing. *"The land furnishes us with beauty and our simple needs," says Lonnie. "After people visit my mom, I hope they remember us as keeping our traditions while making a living," adds Effie. " It's good to show them that anyone can live with just a little if you have to."*

◀ **Larry Holiday exemplifies** the independent spirit of many young Navajos. *"In high school I worked at Gouldings from 5-8 AM, and then from 6-9 PM. I went to school and did homework in between. Today I serve my people as school-community liaison, helping them work with American culture. On weekends I teach visitors about our culture. I guess I'm kind of a two-way-street Navajo!"*

▲ *In a time when most young couples seek the easier life of a city or tribal housing development,* a few turn to the land to reconnect with the life of their ancestors. Lorraine Cly and Jamieson Black have chosen to raise their family near Cly Butte. "Everything is here," says Jamieson, smiling as he strips bark from cedar poles to make a corral, "helping out the family, doing chores, being happy!" "We must carry water, chop wood for heat, and use gas lamps," adds Lorraine. "We could use a generator but we prefer the quiet. We appreciate what nature gives us, and don't take anything for granted."

▲ **Suzie Yazzie began demonstrating rug weaving to tourists at her hogan in the 1940s. She started** weaving at age10 and now, at age 80, she continues to enjoy sharing her art. She is acknowledged as the first valley resident to pioneer tourist home visits. On having visitors she says, "I want them to remember how rugs are made and that I still do it!"

A Look Back in Time

Frank Jackson is known ▶ worldwide as the "Navajo John Wayne." He is the man in the red shirt on horseback, and he can be found almost every day at his family's business at John Ford Point posing for photographs. He inherited the "job" from John Cly (see back cover). "I love the valley and the tourists who come here," he says humbly.

▲ **Daisy Holiday Haycock was photographed by Josef Muench in the early 1960s when** she was about 3 years old. "All I can remember is that we were dressed up and taken places to pose for photos," she says. "This is still the most wonderful place to live!"

Dineh: The People

▲ **N**early 100 years old, Billy Yellow continues **to** serve as a traditional healer. "I'm trying my best to keep the ceremonies alive," he says. Still young at heart he drives, walks briskly, and loves visiting the flea market.

The future of Navajo culture ▲ is at a dynamic crossroads. When today's young, like 3-year old Juanita Perry, grow up, will they know their Navajo language and culture? Living in Monument Valley encourages the young to maintain the Navajo way of life.

◄ **A** top academic student, 16-year old Valentina S. Smith lives in two worlds. "When I put on my Navajo dress, it's like going back in time, to how my great, great, grandparents lived," she says. "Their lives help make me strong."

▲ *Living in a famous landscape offers residents* many varied experiences. "I saw John Wayne when I was a kid herding sheep," states Mark Cly Olds. "They were filming, and I went to their noon buffet 'cause they had food. Later I lived in California for 20 years, but it's like the medicine man said, 'If you stay within the Navajo sacred mountains, you'll be protected.' I wasn't safe there, so here I am."

▲ *"Visitors should know that we have* our own names for the rocks," says Mary Cly Holiday. "In our Navajo language we call the Mittens and Mitchell Butte together, 'those that are standing.'" Navajo names suggest an anima *in the rocks, complementing the Navajo belief that all of nature contains spirit.*

◄ *"I have this little donkey to remind* me how as children we used our donkey to get water," recounts Elsie Mae Cly Begay. "We'd tie metal cans to the saddle, lead the donkey to the spring a few miles away, fill them up, and return home. We did that every few days to have water." A jeweler and family historian, Elsie Mae was featured in the documentary film "Return of Navajo Boy." A granddaughter of Happy and Willie Cly, Elsie Mae has been photographed since the 1930s. Her family worked demonstrating Navajo life ways to tourists.

▲ *The Navajo chief Manuelito believed in education, telling his people to "climb the ladder of education."* Until 1983, the youth of Monument Valley had to endure a 3-4-hour one-way bus ride to attend high school in Blanding, Utah. Today, a completely modern high school integrates American educational practices with traditional Navajo cultural learning. Monument Valley High School students have access to the full range of academic pursuits, sports programs, and computer and college courses.

▲ *Laticia, Victoria, and Sabrina Rodriguez (left to right)* live with their mother Linda on family land at John Ford's Point. Here, they perform pow-wow style dances for special tour groups, sharing the meaning and history of each dance.

◄ *"I know that my heart belongs here," says Alvina* Holiday, age 25. Young, restless, and once wanting to leave the area, Alvina has chosen to remain, care for, and learn weaving from her grandmother Suzie Yazzie.

Youth at Work and Play

◀ **N**avajo basket weavers from the Douglas Mesa/Monument Valley area are revolutionizing their art form with intricate patterns and colors that often illustrate Navajo stories. At work here in her mother's hogan, Joann Johnson weaves a new creation. Other weavers to look for include Sally, Agnes, and Mary Black, as well as Elsie Holiday. Their artistry has turned a single-style craft into fine art.

▲ **B**ased at the high school the ◀ N'dahoo'aah (Re- and New Learning) Center was established to bring the community and generations together. It features Navajo language classes, a student-operated cultural museum, hogan-building workshops, and a dance circle. A prosperous community garden demonstrates water-saving home gardening techniques to area residents. The Churro Sheep Project re-introduces this original breed and explores the growing popularity of using llamas as "sheepdogs."

The Many Moods of Monument Valley

▲ **The Navajo believe that all elements** in nature are endowed with spirit. Navajos view moon, rock, plant, and all other natural phenomena as holding special knowledge that can aid human beings.

▲ **The Mittens and other buttes were originally named** to entice tourists. Seasons' light and weather reveal an ever-changing playground for human imagination. What would you name these marvelous monuments of stone?

This book honors the Monument Valley community and those families who generously offered assistance to photographers Josef Muench and Bruce Hucko. To the Cly, Jackson, Yazzie, Black, and Holiday families, past and present, we extend a heartfelt *aheehe* (Navajo for "thank you").

The land tells many stories. Whether you ▶ listen to a geologist describing history or a Navajo elder re-telling an ancient creation myth, one truth persists — that Monument Valley will inspire people for ages to come.

▲ *The Valley never changes and yet it's always different! This scene taken in 1990 is similar to the 1937 photo on the cover. The 808-foot-high Totem Pole has been scaled and even used in auto commercials. A convertible was slung onto the top by a helicopter! Today the Navajo shy away from such usage of their monument. The formation in behind is called the Yeibichai after dancers of their mythology. Everybody is swept up by the charm of Monument Valley although for vastly different reasons. Beauty is in the eyes of the beholder. Certainly this Valley is a perfect example of that philosophy.*

SUGGESTED READING

BAHTI, MARK. *Southwestern Indian Weaving.* Las Vegas, Nevada: KC Publications, Inc., 2001.

BAHTI, TOM, and MARK BAHTI. *Southwestern Indian Arts & Crafts.* Las Vegas, Nevada: KC Publications, Inc., 1997.

BAHTI, TOM, and MARK BAHTI. *Southwestern Indian Ceremonials.* Las Vegas, Nevada: KC Publications, Inc., 1997.

BAHTI, TOM, and MARK BAHTI. *Southwestern Indian Tribes.* Las Vegas, Nevada: KC Publications, Inc., 1997.

HUCKO, BRUCE. *Southwestern Indian Pottery.* Las Vegas, Nevada: KC Publications, Inc., 1999.

MARTINEAU, LA VAN. *The Rocks Begin to Speak.* Las Vegas, Nevada: KC Publications, Inc., 1973.

MOON, DR. SAMUEL. *Tall Sheep.* Norman, Oklahoma: University of Oklahoma Press, 1992.

The Navajo Treaty – 1868. Las Vegas, Nevada: KC Publications, Inc., 1968.

REED, ALLEN C. *Grand Circle Adventure.* Las Vegas, Nevada: KC Publications, Inc., 1983.

ROSEN, JUDY, and BIFF BAIRD. *I is for Indians of the Southwest.* Las Vegas, Nevada: KC Publications, Inc., 2000.

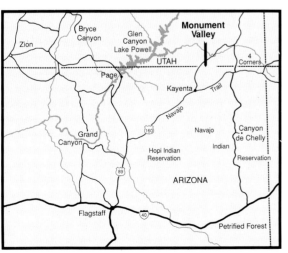

There is so much to see in the Valley. Yet, it ▲
is the dramatic symbols that catch the eye and
are most remembered by the viewers, and their cameras!
The "Totem Pole," the Navajos and their sheep coming
down the dunes, and here we have the "Mittens." Framed
by a well-placed juniper, these "hands-of-time"
welcome you near the entrance to Monument Valley —
or are they saying goodbye as you leave? Perhaps it
may be best said that they stand as friendly signs from the
Navajo people, asking you to return again and again.

◀ **M**onument Valley is at 5,200-foot elevation, north of
Kayenta, Arizona, along the Navajo Trail. The Valley
is along the Arizona-Utah border. Roads are open all
year long, but there is snow during the winter.

61

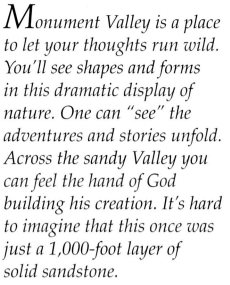

*M*onument Valley is a place to let your thoughts run wild. You'll see shapes and forms in this dramatic display of nature. One can "see" the adventures and stories unfold. Across the sandy Valley you can feel the hand of God building his creation. It's hard to imagine that this once was just a 1,000-foot layer of solid sandstone.

A sculptor was once asked how he carved a horse out of a block of granite. "Simple," he said, "just take away everything that doesn't look like a horse." So God started with one hundred square miles of sandstone and just took away everything that didn't look like Monument Valley! And now it's ours — to appreciate and enjoy. An untouched creation of nature that touches us all.

Full moon and the "King on his Throne," "The Stagecoach," "Bear and the Rabbit," with the "Big Indian" on the right. What a world for a vivid imagination.

▲ *The Valley in all its splendor. Eroded layers of rich red earth, the monuments in their majesty.* *Enough plant life to add touches of green and provide habitat for its little creatures. To top it off, a selection of fluffy clouds. As Josef Muench once commented, "I feel lonely when I don't have any clouds."*

*I*nside back cover: ▶
*The Mittens reach
for the sky at sunrise.*

*B*ack cover: *The Navajo,* ▶
*protector of the Valley.
The Valley, home of the Navajo.*

Created, Designed, and Published in the U.S.A.
Printed by Tien Wah Press (Pte.) Ltd, Singapore
Pre-Press by United Graphic Pte. Ltd